RECLAIMING RADICAL IDEAS IN SCHOOLS

CU01085317

Reclaiming Radical Ideas in the Classroom provides support for every primary school in the provision of Spiritual, Moral, Social and Cultural Development (SMSC), the teaching of British values and preparation for life in modern Britain.

Providing practical and tried-and-tested strategies, this resource will help primary schools work together to create an inclusive environment that focuses on reducing radicalisation and radical ideas. It will support schools in creating an ethos for young children where their questions about the world are explored and answered without fear or discrimination.

Moffat is the author of *No Outsiders in Our School: Teaching the Equality Act in Primary Schools*, which provides teachers with a curriculum that promotes equality for all sections of the community. Using the No Outsiders model as a foundation, this new book complements it by putting emphasis on engaging parent communities in the school ethos.

The resource includes thirteen lesson plans to deliver with children and their parents in school-based workshops, with homework activities to follow. Each lesson is based around a picture book and includes fun activities alongside discussion of issues on individual differences, including race, gender and sexuality. The resource also provides guidance on how to deliver assemblies that support the No Outsiders ethos and how to approach discussing terrorism with children.

This is an invaluable resource for anyone working in a primary school setting, as well as trainee teachers, ITT providers and educational advisors. The aim is to extend the successful No Outsiders ethos beyond the school gates to the community to ensure that we are working together to develop a safe and cohesive British society.

Andrew Moffat is Assistant Head Teacher at a large Primary School in inner city Birmingham. He is the author of *No Outsiders in Our School: Teaching the Equality Act in Primary Schools* (Speechmark 2015) and delivers training on 'No Outsiders' across the country. He has a Masters in Emotional and Behavioural Difficulties and is currently researching the role of schools in reducing radicalisation for a PhD. In 2017 Andrew Moffat was awarded an MBE for services to equality and diversity in education.

RECLAIMING RADICAL IDEAS IN SCHOOLS

Preparing Young Children for Life in Modern Britain

ANDREW MOFFAT

Routledge
Taylor & Francis Group

LONDON AND NEW YORK

First published 2018
by Routledge
2 Park Square, Milton Park, Abingdon, Oxon OX14 4RN

and by Routledge
711 Third Avenue, New York, NY 10017

Routledge is an imprint of the Taylor & Francis Group, an informa business

British Library Cataloguing-in-Publication Data
A catalogue record for this book is available from the British Library

Library of Congress Cataloging-in-Publication Data
A catalog record has been requested

ISBN: 978-1-138-56431-2 (pbk)
ISBN: 978-1-315-12237-3 (ebk)

Typeset in Univers
by Apex CoVantage, LLC

Contents

Figures

Tables

Preface

The Equality Act 2010

The Equality Duty covers the following protected characteristics:

- Age
- Gender reassignment
- Marriage or Civil Partnership
- Pregnancy and maternity
- Disability
- Race- this includes ethnic or national origins, colour or nationality
- Religion or belief- this includes lack of belief
- Sex
- Sexual orientation

(Homeoffice.gov.uk, 2011)

The website www.equalitiesprimary.com links to assembly pictures, training opportunities and updated lesson plans for No Outsiders.

The UN Convention on the rights of a child

Article 2

"The convention applies to every child without discrimination, whatever their ethnicity, gender, religion, language, abilities or any other status. Whatever they think or say, whatever their family background."

Article 14

"Every child has the right to think and believe what they choose and also to practise their religion, as long as they are not stopping other people from enjoying their rights."

Article 30

"Every child has the right to learn and use the language, customs and religion of their family, whether or not these are shared by the majority of the people in the country where they live."

(Rights Respecting Schools: unicef.org.uk/rrsa)

"Everyone is an insider, there are no outsiders whatever their beliefs, whatever their colour, whatever their gender or sexuality." – Archbishop Desmond Tutu, February 2004

Acknowledgements

Thanks to Hazel Pulley, David Williams and the brilliant staff at Parkfield Community School, Excelsior Trust, for piloting this resource and being so enthusiastic and encouraging.

Many people have been huge supporters of No Outsiders in the last two years and I want to thank everyone who has helped the work along the way. In particular I want to thank Amanda Daniels, Dawn Latham and Bullying Reduction Action Group supported by Birmingham City Council (www.stopbullyinginbrum.co.uk).

Thanks to the original No Outsiders team (2006–2008) for starting me on my way.

Thanks to Speechmark and Routledge for continued support.

Thanks to www.letterboxlibrary.com for supplying all the picture books used in the No Outsiders resources.

Thanks to Razia Butt and Unicef Rights Respecting.

Thanks to Rabiyah Latif for expanding my understanding of faith.

Thanks to Cate for inspirational teaching.

Finally, thanks to my wonderful husband, David, for pretending to listen.

Chapter One

INTRODUCTION

Introduction

This book helps to meet the challenges faced by schools and their safeguarding duties in the 21st century. Our children are regularly exposed to news stories and events that may instigate feelings of uncertainty and fear, and schools must be confident in the narrative they are promoting. How do we respond to an eight year old in 2017 questioning why a man killed twenty-three people at a concert in Manchester, or why another man killed five people on Westminster Bridge, drove a lorry into crowds in Nice or drove a van into a group of worshipers outside a mosque in London? Following the Charlie Hebdo massacre in 2015 a child asked me in a Year 5 assembly, "Why do the terrorists do this? Why do they kill people?" Children hear these news stories and are searching for answers to make sense of the world. We cannot shield children or wrap them in cotton wool, nor can we leave their conclusions to chance; rather schools need to be confident in providing clear but age-appropriate responses to those questions. A carefully nurtured school ethos can enable news events to be discussed within the confines of a safe school environment, but schools need to create that safe and secure ethos. In this environment, dialogue is encouraged and a clear narrative is developed.

The Prevent Duty states all schools must have "due regard to the need to prevent people from being drawn in to terrorism" (HM Gov, 2015, p. 4) and recommends schools "provide a safe space in which children, young people and staff can understand the risks associated with terrorism and develop the knowledge and skills to be able to challenge extremist arguments" (HM Gov, 2015, p. 5). I wrote *No Outsiders in Our School: Teaching the Equality Act in Primary Schools* in 2015 and since then the world has changed dramatically; in the last two years we have seen a rise in terrorist attacks across Europe and the UK. In the original No Outsiders book I referenced radicalisation briefly; however since then I have been developing the resource with a specific aim to prevent young people from being drawn in to terrorism, rather than as a resource simply to promote equality and diversity. Of course the two discourses go hand in hand; we reduce radical ideas by promoting community cohesion through an understanding and celebration of diversity and equality. To advocate radical ideas is to reject the ideals and values of community cohesion. The No Outsiders strategy ensures an equality ethos is clear from the outset; we not only respond to radical ideas if and when they emerge, but more importantly we proactively promote an alternative narrative to reduce that risk in the first place.

In a nutshell, schools need to be consistently and confidently promoting an ethos where all children feel safe and secure in the knowledge they belong and their family belongs; that despite their differences to the person in the seat next to them in class, both students are welcome in the school and wider society. Schools must demonstrate examples of community cohesion working successfully; we need to be identifying and promoting examples of successful community cohesion and diversity around us. More importantly where community cohesion is understood to be failing, schools need to be responding quickly and encouraging students to find solutions that are cohesive, not divisive.

In this work I make no apology for use of the word "promote" because that is exactly what schools must do to provide the alternative narrative needed. An alternative narrative is needed to one in which terrorism, building walls or deportation are put forward as responses to difference. Why should schools promote an alternative narrative? When media investigated the background of Khalid Massood, the man who killed five people and injured fifty in London, March 2017, they found a boy who was the only black child in a 1970s class of white children, who had a nickname, "Black Ade". Asim Riaz, a solicitor from Birmingham talking about the attack, says, "The problem is disenfranchised youths . . . . they feel they don't belong in the UK even though they were born here. They feel rejected by their country . . . it's about feeling ostracised" (Sherwood and Pidd, 2017).

This resource emphasises exploring attitudes around immigration and community cohesion. This is in direct response to the rise in terrorist attacks in the UK and Europe and also to two major political events that have taken place recently – Brexit and the election of Donald Trump.

In 2016, Donald Trump was elected following a campaign that included calls to build a wall to keep out of the US people who were different. Following the election an article in *The Independent* highlighted some of the divisive policies that took him to the White House,

> **A crackdown on illegal immigration was the early centrepiece of Mr Trump's campaign, earning him ranks of supporters and opponents alike. From day one he has vowed to build a wall the length of the US-Mexican border – for which he insists he will force Mexico to pay – and to deport the estimated 11 million undocumented migrants living in the US.**
>
> (Walker, 2016)

Children were aware of these views, and when Trump was elected I wrote an article for *The Guardian* online in which I described the response from many Muslim pupils at my school; "He hates Muslims," one child said. "He's going to stop Muslims going to America" (Moffat, 2016). I felt at the time there was a need to write a second volume of No Outsiders to specifically address the fears I was dealing with on a daily basis from the children in my school, about the emerging world around them. The children needed to feel safe and needed to hear that they belonged. Furthermore they needed to appreciate and understand the situations that existed for other children who may be seeking that safety and belonging in a migrant situation. I wanted to develop an ethos of empathy for people who found themselves in these terrible situations rather than fear. At the very least I wanted to find ways to talk about these situations with children and adults rather than brush them under the carpet.

Earlier in the same year the UK voted out of the European Union. Ukip famously released a "Breaking Point" campaign poster depicting hundreds of migrants walking in line. At the time Chancellor George Osbourne spoke about his fears for the repercussions that could arise from the campaign; Ukip were, he said, "whipping up division," and referenced the Breaking Point poster as having, "echoes of literature used in the 1930s" (Riley-Smith, 2016). This was an interesting time to be a teacher in a school with a strong No Outsiders ethos where we talked all the time about everyone being welcome. I heard conversations at the time that openly talked about "shutting the gates" and expressing concern about "too many Romanians" coming over to the UK.

The reported spike in hate crimes in schools following these campaigns is extremely worrying; one year on the *TES* reported,

- In May last year – in the middle of the Brexit referendum campaign – the number of police reports of hate crimes and hate incidents in schools rose by 89% compared with the same month in 2015.

- During the summer and autumn terms in 2016 – when the Brexit referendum took place and Donald Trump won the US presidential election – the number of hate crimes and hate incidents in schools increased by 48% compared with the same period in 2015. (Busby, 2017)

Where the prevailing ideas in society suggest a trend in rejections of community cohesion, schools are in an ideal position to proactively set a radical opposite trend. This resource uses thirteen picture books, and five of them specifically focus on immigration or on people from different backgrounds sharing the same space. The aim is very clear – to talk about immigration in a way that allows children to explore attitudes and develop an understanding of messages of division and messages of collaboration. Where radical ideas exist the aim is to nurture an alternative understanding; this resource is championing community cohesion.

Schools must ensure that all young people and families feel they belong. The essence of a No Outsiders ethos is just that; we teach children that we are all different but we all belong here, wherever that is. Furthermore we can all get on, working alongside each other and respecting each other in our diverse, colourful, vibrant, brilliant community. Dialogue is a key element to our success; people can change ideas and mind-sets, which is why we need to start involving parents in this ethos, learning together and creating our school and community ethos together.

This is not a woolly liberal narrative where we just talk about being kind to one another; rather this is a proactive and robust ethos whose aim is to convince children (and parents) of the benefits that arise from living in a diverse Britain. Children may be forming ideas about diversity and equality from sources that are not always conducive to cohesion. It is the schools' role to be absolutely clear, from the moment children enter the gates, about how we see equality and diversity and how immersion in those values prepares children for the world outside those gates; it prepares them for life in modern Britain.

Children need a resilient inner core; a belief or understanding that they belong in the UK and furthermore that diversity works for them and for the greater society. We must teach children to belong and to want to belong; today people are black and British, white and British, Christian and British, Muslim and British, gay and British etc.; our UK needs to be united in its diversity. The MP Jo Cox who was murdered in 2016 famously said in her first address to the Houses of Parliament, "We are far more united and have far more in common than that which divides us" (Cox, 2017), and that quote is the very foundation of the No Outsiders thread. Our role is to demonstrate this to our young children in schools – diversity and community cohesion works and schools need to be confidently and consistently providing examples.

This volume should be read in conjunction with the first No Outsiders resource (Moffat, 2015). The No Outsiders ethos described here is no different to the ethos described in that book. The No Outsiders ethos teaches children there are 'No Outsiders' in our school because we are all 'insiders', thereby excluding no one. The Equality Act 2010 is used as a baseline and to reference British values and British law. The protected characteristics listed in the Equality Act 2010 provide a framework for schools where children and young people learn about the difference and diversity that exists in their classroom and in the UK. Put simply, we first recognise difference and then we celebrate it. Children in early years can learn, "I like apples and you like pears and we can still be friends," and this is extended as they grow older to recognising how our protected characteristics make us different and we can still get along.

The imaginative and engaging picture books used in the original No Outsiders resource, such as *Red Rockets and Rainbow Jelly* by Sue Heap and Nick Sharratt, *This Is Our House* by Michael Rosen and *The Island* by Armin Greder, encourage children to develop a real understanding of equality and diversity and, crucially, to feel confident in the benefits that arise from a diverse society. The aim of stories listed in the No Outsiders book list is to develop pupils' confidence in their own differences and acceptance of the diversity and difference that exists in others. The Prevent Duty calls on schools to develop these skills in pupils; "Schools can encourage pupils to develop positive character traits through PSHE such as resilience, determination, self-esteem and confidence" (HM Gov, 2015, p. 8).

In my own school, in our Ofsted report, May 2016, the inspectors were very clear in their recognition of the No Outsiders programme and its impact on the school:

> *The provision for pupils' spiritual, moral, social and cultural development is a key strength of the school. Fundamental British values are actively promoted through the school's work on "No outsiders in our school," which develops pupils' understanding of how the Equality Act relates to and affects them. As a result, pupils celebrate diversity and are respectful towards others, including those with different beliefs, sexuality, gender or culture. One pupil spoke for many when she told inspectors, "everyone is an insider in our school, there are no outsiders, whatever their beliefs, whatever their colour, gender or sexuality."*
>
> (HM Gov, 2016)

I have no idea which child gave the Ofsted inspectors the quote in their report but I was not surprised to read it; the No Outsiders thread runs throughout the school and children are very confident when questioned about it. This is because all staff talk about No Outsiders at every opportunity – in lessons, assemblies and relating it to everyday incidents. I always say to visitors to our school, "You can ask any child we pass in the corridor about No Outsiders and you will get an answer."

The aim now is to extend the No Outsiders ethos and use it to foster community cohesion through parent/child workshops. The parents in my own school are very supportive of the work we are doing around No Outsiders and are happy for me to use their words and film footage of their conversations as part of my training for teachers. However, I am constantly reflecting on the impact of the work and I am unsure whether the ethos we have created in school is always mirrored outside the school walls. I am reminded of a quote from the Head of our school in an article in *The Guardian* which focused on our work around LGBT equality:

> *Everyone knows we respect Islam here. One parent asked if he could not contradict what the school said. I told him that whatever parents said*

in the home was their decision but it's lovely that the children will hear both views.

(Lightfoot, 2016)

I often use this quote when talking about the impact of our work and how we have managed to work with our parent community because we have reached an understanding, where we teach there are simply different opinions and ideas. We teach that it is ok to hear and talk about different ideas and we can still have respect for one another if we disagree. We balance the two views about faith and about LGBT equality; both views exist and both can co-exist; it's good that children understand in life there are different views and we can talk about different views and still get along. A parent interviewed in the same article continues:

I'd rather my children hear it at school. When they are at home we teach them that in our culture gay is not allowed but we respect people who are different from us and hope they too will respect us and the boundaries of our religion.

(Lightfoot, 2016)

What these quotes suggest is that in the infancy of No Outsiders we have enabled conversations with our parent community about LGBT equality that may never before have taken place. This is an achievement in itself and a worthy beginning, but two years further on, questions need to be asked about the effectiveness of the work when it is confined to working behind the school walls. Are we teaching children to say one thing when in school and another at home or in their local community, and if so, is this real change? Are we really engaging with the community on new ideas?

Where the prevailing narrative around children is one of discrimination based on difference, it is time to reclaim radical ideas. We are becoming the radical ones; ideas of LGBT equality or race equality, for example, may seem radical to some members of our community but we need to work with those members to come to an ethos of tolerance. "Foster good relations between different people," says the

Equality Act 2010 (Government Equalities Office, 2013, p. 1). The Ofsted handbook for maintained schools (2016) also sets out clear guidelines:

> *138. The social development of pupils is shown by their acceptance and engagement with the fundamental British values of democracy, the rule of law, individual liberty and mutual respect and tolerance of those with different faiths and beliefs; they develop and demonstrate skills and attitudes that will allow them to participate fully in and contribute positively to life in modern Britain.*
>
> (Gov.uk, 2016, p. 35)

The radical ideas No Outsiders promotes are based on tolerance and acceptance of those with different beliefs, culture or lifestyle and the aim is to turn tolerance into acceptance and then celebration. The word 'tolerance' is often criticised in this context because it suggests one 'puts up with' someone different rather than accepts them. However, I see tolerance as being a realistic stop on the way to acceptance. Where someone has little experience of a specific protected characteristic, tolerance may come first. Tolerance is a good thing and can lead to full acceptance through experience and dialogue. A No Outsiders ethos argues that people can change and dialogue is an essential element of community cohesion. In the picture book *This Is Our House* by Michael Rosen, the character George changes his mind after discriminating against groups of people; he changes through a new experience and realises he was wrong. We can all change.

Parents have the biggest influence on their children's upbringing so it makes sense to work with the parent community on these ideas. We want to avoid children receiving mixed messages about community cohesion, so the aim of this resource is to invite parents to join with us and learn together. Of course many of our parents already share our views about equality and diversity and by taking part in these workshops we are merely showcasing the language used in school that can be reinforced at home. It's wonderful when children see their parents agreeing with a school ethos. We can develop a common language around equalities to be used by children and parents alike which fosters true community cohesion for the future generation.

In conclusion, the aim in this book is to use the No Outsiders framework described in the first volume and broaden the impact to parents and the community. The lesson plans in this volume are focused on children working with parents to develop their understanding and commitment to equalities. Rather than lesson plans for the classroom, these are lesson plans for child-parent workshops with homework, to reinforce the message outside the school gates.

The No Outsiders model has been proved to be effective inside the classroom (HM Gov, 2016). The aim now is to develop that effectiveness to the community. In this way we engage with parents and bring parents with us, so the core ideas of community cohesion we want children to sign up to are understood and nurtured in both the home and community and in turn, in society at large.

Chapter Two

RESPONDING TO TERRORIST ATTACKS USING SCHOOL ASSEMBLIES

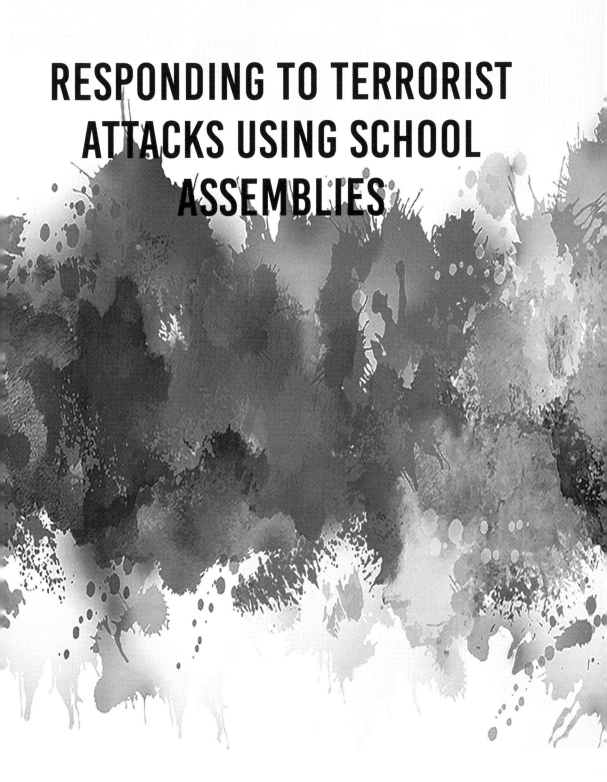

Responding to terrorist attacks using school assemblies

School assemblies give schools a perfect opportunity to take the No Outsiders ethos and make it real and relevant. I use assembly pictures taken from up-to-date news events and stories to demonstrate to children every day that it's not just us who believes in No Outsiders; lots of people around the world agree with us. There are people right now in all parts of the globe who are working together despite their differences and diversity.

The assembly pictures are a crucial part of the No Outsiders resource because they reduce the risk of the ethos becoming faded and generic. As children reach Year 6, if they have been exposed to the lesson plans since early years we need vehicles to keep the message fresh. News stories are a valuable resource, taking the ethos out of the classroom and demonstrating No Outsiders can be found everywhere. The stories encourage children to relate their learning to news stories they hear every day; we are building resilience to the current climate where prevailing stories often challenge the No Outsiders message.

Following the tragic events in Manchester, May 2017, a child in Year 6 at my school wrote a letter to me. In the letter the child describes their response to the event but also links the response to No Outsiders in order to make sense of it:

> *The suicide bomb attack in Manchester was wrong but also very rare. It killed a lot of people and the bomber himself. It caused a lot of damage but some good has come from it as people are coming together and helping each other. One homeless man ran in to the scene of the bomb helping children and adults. As a thank you people decided to donate money to him. It is like no outsiders as no one is rejected.*

This letter shows the child has the resilience and skills to make sense of the tragedy. They acknowledge the tragic loss of life and make their response clear. However, they also look for the positive community response in the aftermath and link the 'coming together' of the community to the No Outsiders ethos. This is exactly how I respond to terrorist attacks, using assembly pictures.

I get many of my assembly pictures from *Huffington Post* (www.huffingtonpost. com) and I run an assembly picture blog at www.equalitiesprimary.com, where each week I blog about a new picture with discussion points and questions to ask. The pictures are wide ranging in subject matter but the conclusion is always the same; "How is this story about No Outsiders?" The aim is to take the lessons learned in the No Outsiders curriculum (Moffat, 2015) and link the learning to real-life events that happened in the last week. In this way we are showing that No Outsiders is all around us and happening right now.

There have been some fantastic pictures to use over the past year with heart-warming stories that demonstrate a No Outsiders ethos. Often stories go viral very quickly, which we are then able to use to demonstrate the interest and support that exists in humanity for a No Outsiders ethos and a world where community cohesion is celebrated.

The story of the young man in Toronto holding hands with a stranger on a bus who had cerebral palsy and asked for help; the story of a grown-up son singing old songs with his elderly dad in his car to provide respite from Alzheimer's; the story of the trans woman returning to work following her transition to find flowers and a card on her desk from colleagues showing their acceptance and support; the story of a boy standing in front of an anti-gay march in Brazil, arms outstretched to protest against hate. There are hundreds of brilliant stories and pictures we can use to tap in to our ethos, showing successful examples of diversity and community cohesion working around the world.

An example of how to use the images:

> *As children enter the hall have a picture up on the board. Children sit and contemplate the picture as the hall fills, thinking of explanations for what might be the subject matter or where it was taken; what is happening.*

I used a story by Taylor Pittman (2017) on *Huffington Post* about a high school in Florida where students set up a 'We dine together' club to ensure students do not sit alone during lunch. If a student is found sitting alone, a 'We dine together' member makes an introduction and sits with the student. Student Denis Estimon is one of four students who set up the club and explains, "If we don't try and go make that change, who's going to do it?" (Pittman, 2017). Estimon came to the US from Haiti in first grade and describes how alone he felt upon arrival when he started school. Estimon's actions now ensure no one at his school feels like an outsider. What would Estimon think about our school? Would he agree with our No Outsiders message? What can we learn from Estimon? Why is this story about No Outsiders?

But how do we respond when children have heard about challenging and upsetting news stories before they enter the assembly hall, and the stories suggest there is a harsh reality in our world where community cohesion is threatened? The aim of the No Outsiders ethos is to develop a clear narrative in schools where children recognise, understand and support diversity and community cohesion; however there are times when news events contradict the narrative we are promoting. In the aftermath of a terrorist attack, children are right to question us; "You tell us No Outsiders is everywhere but look what just happened!" We are promoting ideas about a world where different people get on and work together, so how do we explain acts of terror?

I struggled to come up with responses for acts of terrorism and first used this response following the Charlie Hebdo massacre in January 2015. I have been using the same response ever since. The basic principle works if the school has a clear No Outsiders ethos:

> When talking about tragic events such as terror attacks to young people, explain that we know not everyone agrees with us and 'No Outsiders'. Some people want one race, one religion, one kind of person. This is the opposite to us; we want lots of different races, different religions, different kinds of people. That is why it is so important that we spread our 'No Outsiders' message and keep talking about it. If you meet someone who doesn't understand about diversity and difference, or who does not understand about 'No Outsiders', talk to them.

I used two assembly pictures to talk about the attack in Manchester in 2017 and published them on the assembly picture blog link on www.equalitiesprimary.com. The first post was immediately after the attack on the morning of 22 May when news was still coming in about tragic events. A story emerged about people using Twitter to offer free beds and food to those stranded in the city looking for loved ones or not able to get home. Using an image of rolling tweets taken from www.bbc.co.uk, I explained the story and then asked the following questions:

Why are hundreds of people offering rooms to stay in?

When people offer rooms, are they saying "Men only" or "Christians only" or "Able-bodied people only" or "Straight people only"? Why not?

What does this show about people in Manchester?

What can we learn from the people offering rooms?

Why is this about No Outsiders?

The vigil held in Manchester that night provided another opportunity to talk about the attack and allow children to form a response, highlighting the positive examples of community cohesion that were pouring out of Manchester. Showing an image of the huge vigil, with quotes from the Bishop of Manchester and a poet who read out an ode to the city, my second post asked the following discussion questions:

- Who came to the vigil?

- Were there people of different faith and culture at the vigil? Were people with disabilities, who are LGBT, of different ethnicities, genders and ages present? What does this show us about Manchester?

- What does the Bishop mean when he says "We are Manchester" (Slater, 2017)?

- What does the poet mean when he says, "If you're looking from history then yeah we're a wealth" (Slater, 2017)?

- What can we learn from Manchester and this vigil?

- Why is this story about No Outsiders?

Both assemblies ended with a moment of reflection to think about those affected by the attack in Manchester and also about what we can do in our school and our community to make sure positive ideas about diversity and difference spread.

I have responded to many tragic events in a similar way to the one described above. My aim is twofold: first to show respect to those affected by the tragedy and allow a time of reflection in my school; second to encourage the children in my school to feel they have a responsibility to develop a response to the event. I am teaching children to be part of the world and to care about events around them, moreover to understand that their response today can affect future events. Our community is made up of each of us; we either strive for and build cohesion, or we retreat and let it fail. My aim is for children to choose the former option.

Chapter Three

WORKING WITH PARENTS: THE NO OUTSIDERS WORKSHOPS

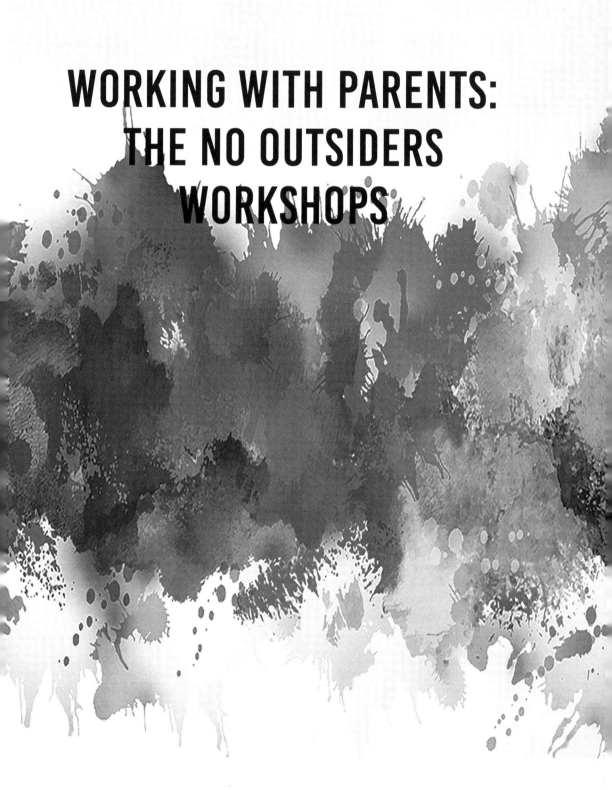

Working with parents: the No Outsiders workshops

I have written thirteen lesson plans to deliver as parent and child workshops in school. The aim of these workshops is to work with our parent community to develop a common language for promoting equality and diversity. We want the equality ethos that we have created inside the school gates to permeate the surrounding community where different ideas about equality and diversity may, or may not, exist.

In my own school before we started teaching No Outsiders we held parent meetings where we shared the thirty-five picture books in the scheme, but those meetings took place two years ago and we don't feel the need to repeat them, as the scheme is now embedded in the school. When new arrivals are shown around the school we explain about No Outsiders, and the many displays both inside and outside the school make the ethos clear. There have been no complaints or questions about any part of the scheme from parents for the whole of this academic year; parents know about the ethos and accept it, or at least accept that it is taught in the school.

The time is right to extend the No Outsiders ethos beyond the classroom. As a school, we are proud and confident of our equality work and the question is, where do we go now? How do we progress?

The resource uses thirteen picture books, different to the ones listed in the original No Outsiders scheme, and provides lesson plans for workshops where children take part with their parents/carers (see chapter 6 for full book list and plans). There are two lesson plans for each year group Year 1–Year 6 and one lesson plan for EYFS. The subject matter in the books will be familiar to those who have taught the No Outsiders resource previously; these are books that allow students to explore solutions to situations where characters feel different. *Odd Dog Out* by Rob Biddulph, for example, is a perfect vehicle for this work and even mentions a character feeling like an 'outsider'.

Delivering the workshops

I led a staff inset and showed everyone the two books and plans for each year group in order for people to get an understanding of how the resource progressed through the school. I asked teachers, rather than me, to lead the workshops so that parents saw their own class teachers as confident ambassadors for the work. We set up a timetable for each class, and sent out the following letter to each class one week before their workshop. In some classes children wrote personal invitations for their parents to reinforce the letter. I took responsibility for sending out all the letters and preparing all the workshops on the day; although the teachers led the sessions, I remained in the room.

Dear Parent/Carer,

You are invited to join a 'No Outsiders' lesson with your child.

This term we are holding workshops in school to prepare children for life in modern Britain and we want our parents to join in. In the workshops we will read a picture book together and talk about the characters before playing a game about the story. We will then do a small art activity based on the book and your child will be given a small piece of work to complete later with you at home.

The No Outsiders workshop for class _____ is on _____

Please enter school through the main building. We look forward to seeing you at the workshop.

Many thanks,

At the start of each session the teacher remained in the classroom while I collected the parents who were waiting in the school reception, having signed in. I led the parents into the classroom and they sat next to their child at their table. I opened each session by thanking the parents for coming and explaining why we were doing these workshops; explaining that we talk all the time in school about No Outsiders and our children are very confident about that, and now we wanted to work with the parents so that they were also confident about the ethos and knew what we were teaching. I asked the children to explain to their adult what No Outsiders was all about and then we fed back to the class. The class teachers then took over and delivered the session, but I remained in the room to support.

For the purpose of piloting this book, we did all the workshops within a seven-week half-term. However, in future we will spread the workshops throughout the year. The first workshop we did was for EYFS, using *A Busy Day for Birds* by Lucy Cousins. We invited parents from a teaching group of twenty children, and the day before the workshop the class teacher reminded parents at the gate about the workshop. On the day, ten parents came, which I was positive about as it was the very first workshop. We made the decision at this stage that we would only keep children in the room whose parents came to the session; other children worked in another class for the duration of the session. In some later sessions we chose to keep all children in the classroom rather than exclude those whose parents were not able to attend.

The atmosphere in the room was very positive and although during this workshop no parents joined in with the bird actions, the children loved the activity and the parents clearly enjoyed seeing their children happy. Interestingly the children were keyed in from the very beginning about the birds being different, and that being a good thing. The parents enjoyed creating the birds pictures with their child and all completed their homework activity which was handed in the next day.

I led the parents out at the end of the workshop and asked how they felt the session went. All were very positive and said they would come again. One dad remarked how important he felt the message was; that we are all different but we can get along.

The second workshop was for a Year 4 class using *Last Stop on Market Street* by Matt De La Pena. Eleven parents came to the workshop and again the atmosphere was expectant, if a little cautious. The class teacher led the workshop and children discussed the story, remarking how diverse the characters are. All the parents and children made labels to describe their diversity and among the labels we had Bengali

Muslim, Somali Muslim, asthmatic, wears glasses, sister, mum, good at knitting, housewife, carer, a singer. The bus role play was great fun and everyone joined in; one mum sat at the side saying she was a wheelchair user and parents came back to help her on the bus. At the end of the role play the teacher collected the labels as tickets and stuck them on a large piece of card. She then asked, "What should we do with these labels?" and there was a short discussion. I was about to suggest we display them to show how diverse we are in our class, when a mum said we don't need labels and we should bin them. People agreed so I went with the group. It was great to have the discussion and good for me to reflect and change my plan mid-flow, allowing parents to influence the conclusion.

As we left, one mum told me she felt this work was important. She said, "People think it's all about religion and it's not; it's about so much more." Another asked if we could have the workshops after school in future so that parents who worked could attend, as she had taken time off work to come and she wanted to come to the next one.

We held the second Year 4 workshop a week later, for *Odd Dog Out* by Rob Biddulph, and ten parents attended. Three parents from the first week returned and there were seven new parents. The book proved very popular and everyone joined in the discussion about the dog being different and feeling like an outsider. All parents got involved creating hats and children were very proud of their joint creations. It occurred to me during the session that this workshop was giving these children half an hour of undivided parent attention, working on an art project together, which is something many may not get to experience often. I started rewriting all the plans to use art as an activity in all the sessions from here on, and all were successful as parents and children joined together creating images.

I got hold of thirty sets of paint pallets to make painting in the classroom as simple and mess-free as possible. I kept them together and took them to each workshop, taking them away at the end. I recommend whoever is running the workshops does this rather than asking teachers to set out paint pots and water. We want things to be as easy as possible.

In the session in Year 3 for *Ice in the Jungle*, the group made welcome posters in Norwegian to ensure their refugee polar bear was made to feel she belonged. I made the unfortunate mistake of asking a parent directly to create a 'Welcome' sign and after 10 minutes when I returned to the table, he had not made a start. "My dad's not very good at writing," explained his daughter. I felt mortified and immediately found another task for the parent. I learned it is crucial not to assume adults have skills because unwittingly my actions made that dad feel like an outsider! In future I will ask for volunteers rather than allocate tasks.

We read *My Friend Jamal* in Year 2 and all the parents were very happy to answer questions about their likes, dislikes and individual histories. The teacher put an emphasis on her class being detectives and finding out information by asking questions, which they entered into with great enthusiasm, and I amended the plan to put more focus on this section. While delivering *Under the Same Sky* in Year 1, I noticed parents nodding in agreement during the story as we reinforced the central message – 'we are different but we live together'. The workshop happened to coincide with the tragic attack at the mosque in Finsbury Park, June 2017, and afterwards a dad shook my hand and said to me as we left, "It's very important, what you are doing at this time." The second Year 1 session the following week had double the number of parents attend which was wonderful; clearly word had got out. As we were piloting the workshops I was working with only one class at this stage in each year group, and I had a complaint from a parent in another class asking why they weren't having a 'No Outsiders' workshop; clearly word was spreading in a positive way.

The second Year 1 session uses one of two books in the resource that has an LGBT angle; *Spacegirl Pukes* by Katy Watson tells the story of a girl who vomits everywhere, spreading her germs to her two mums and the cat, before jetting off in her space rocket. My focus is twofold for this session; gender equality and different families working together. The role play for this session was great and children were overjoyed pretending to vomit over their adult. The experiences I outline in my first book (Moffat, 2015) still gave me cause for reflection before using LGBT books with parents, but I was reassured that parents were fully supportive and no one batted an eyelid about the two mums in the story and our focus on the different families in the plenary that exist in the UK today.

The same reaction followed the second story with an LGBT focus which appears in the Year 5 workshop based on *Stella Brings the Family* by Miriam B Schiffer.

My focus for this story is on the school being inclusive to ensure children with two dads or two mums are not made to feel like outsiders at mothers' or fathers' day celebrations. The parents in the room joined in the discussions and a grandad was more concerned about the way his grandson painted him with a large belly during the art activity than about the two dads in the story. As we left I asked the grandad what he thought of the lesson and he paused before saying, "Well, it's very different from when I was at school . . . but I think it's a good thing."

Two books stood out for me during the workshops, *My Name Is Not Refugee* by Kate Milner and *The Journey* by Francesca Sanna, both exploring attitudes around migrants and refugees. The children and parents took very seriously the naming ceremony in the workshop for *My Name Is Not Refugee* and took great care with their name paintings. For *The Journey*, we had more parents attend than in any other workshop, possibly because it was one of the last we did and people were talking about them. Both workshops enabled us to hold thought-provoking and empathetic discussions about refugee experiences related to our own lives. In both workshops the parents and children sat attentive and engaged throughout.

For *The Journey* we gave out copies of the front cover to annotate which we spent ten minutes on, but the discussion demonstrated that there could have been much more time spent on this. As we passed the 'safe bowl' around the class, the groups showed respect and listened to every contribution despite there being over fifty people squeezed in to the room. Comments from the children about what made them feel safe included,

"There is no war to harm us."

"I feel safe because I'm with my mother and she'll protect me even if I'm struggling."

"School makes me feel safe."

At the end of the session I felt it had gone so well with positive comments from parents on the way out that I sent an evaluation form home to ask for comments in order to inform the next round of 'No Outsiders' workshops. Comments that came back from parents included,

"I would encourage my children to read and understand the meaning of today's book. I like the way the book explained to us about immigration to another life."

"It was nice to have a parents meeting about no outsiders because we should always work together."

"It was very helpful because it helped me understand what no outsiders is."

"It will help my child in the future."

On the evaluation I asked, "Some people might think children in primary school are too young for lessons like this, what do you think?" A dad replied,

"I don't believe that's true. I believe today children are capable to adapt to information very quickly and if you listen to them they will talk about it every day."

I regret now not giving out parent evaluations for the other workshops, as I'm sure we would have got some very positive comments back. Below is a copy of the questions I asked on the evaluation that I would use in future.

- What did you think about the story book and its suitability for the session?

- How did you feel about the session and the activities overall?

- Some people might think children in primary schools are too young for lessons like this, what do you think?

- What is your opinion of the No Outsiders ethos following the workshop?

- Any further comments

Chapter Four

ANSWERING CHALLENGING QUESTIONS

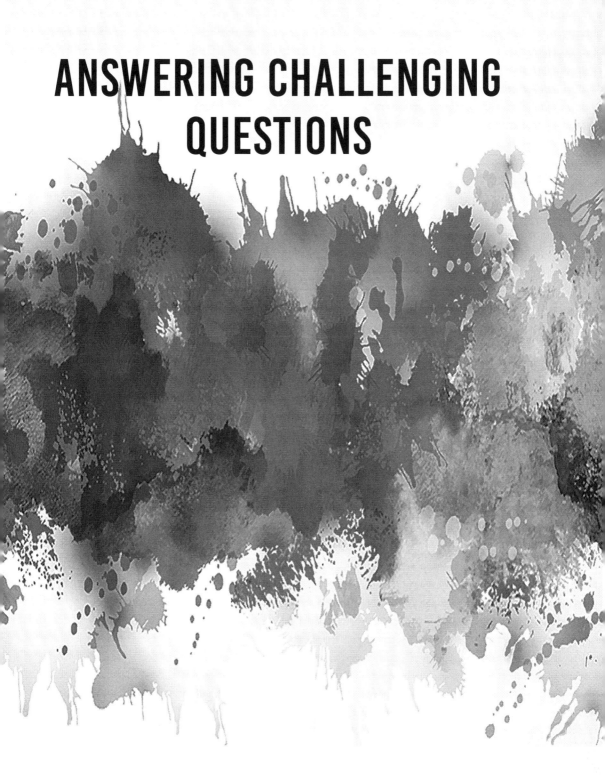

Answering challenging questions

When my school first piloted the No Outsiders resource, we faced many challenging conversations with some parents who were not happy in particular with the perceived focus on LGBT equality. These questions are listed in the original resource with our answers we used at the time (Moffat, 2015), and I am happy to say when we started the 'No Outsiders' parent workshops listed in this resource, there was absolutely no negative response or any questioning from any parent.

What this demonstrates is that as a school we have been able to engage with our parent community in our equalities work. Our parents trust us, support us and have come with us. I believe this is because we held our small parent meetings at the very beginning to involve our parents and carry them with us. We have come a long way as a school in two years.

My experience therefore to deliver this work successfully is to start with the 'No Outsiders' resource and introduce this resource a year or two later as an extension to develop the work with parents.

We did not have any challenging questions here, but it may be the case that in a different community schools receive more challenges around the issues of immigration and equality. Unlike the questions posed in my last book, these are not real questions I have been asked, but I have tried to think of the most difficult questions I could be asked and how I would answer.

Why are we doing this work when we don't have immigrants in our school?
We are preparing our children for life in modern Britain (which is an Ofsted requirement). As they grow up and go to college or university or in their work life they are going to meet people who are different to them. We have to prepare them for that; they aren't only going to be working with people of the same faith or skin colour.

Are you saying we should just welcome anyone into the country?
We are saying that in our school there are No Outsiders and that means everyone is welcome in our school. We want every child to feel safe and feel that they belong.

We are encouraging discussions about refugees and the situations that some people experience, but we are not telling children how to think. Children can make up their own minds about political issues as they grow older; we are giving them the skills to ask questions, think about different viewpoints and exchange dialogue.

Why are you talking about terrorism to my child?

Children hear about terrorism from the news or from adult discussions and they are often frightened about the stories they hear. When there is a terrorist attack children always ask questions in class, and we need as a staff to have a consistent and appropriate response so that our children feel safe in school. Our aim is to allow children to explore feelings about these events and talk about them in a safe environment. Children look for answers to make sense of the world and by talking about 'No Outsiders' we are showing them one way of thinking. It's good for children to hear different viewpoints and understand that not everyone feels the same way about an event.

I don't want my child learning about different faiths

At our school we follow the Equality Act 2010, which is British law and says that a person should not face discrimination because of their faith. We need to prepare our children for life in modern Britain (which is an Ofsted requirement) where they are going to meet, work and live alongside different people, some of whom will practise different faith. Our children need to understand there are different faiths and beliefs in the UK today and that's what makes the UK a great place to live.

When facing challenging questions from parents, keep coming back to the Equality Act 2010 and British law. Unicef Rights Respecting is also a valuable tool to use as both No Outsiders and Rights Respecting back each other up. Our children regularly quote Article 2, which they remember form their classroom charters (www.unicef. org/rrsa). I also quote Ofsted, in particular paragraphs 136–139, which are about spiritual, moral, social and cultural development. Schools can also quote the teachers standards.

When we first engaged with our Muslim parents on teaching about LGBT equality, we had many challenging discussions about how some of our parents could align this equality with their belief that homosexuality was 'wrong'. What we agreed together was that the children in school could hear both views and the beauty of living in the UK was that people can hold different views yet still show each other respect and live alongside each other. There is a balance here; those are two opposing views but we can balance them and children can hear both of them; after all both those views and ideas exist and we can't deny one of them.

What we have found as we have worked with our children and parents over the last two years on our 'No Outsiders' ethos is that attitudes towards LGBT equality have softened. I came out in school as a gay man in October 2015 to no response from the parent community. This was done at the right time, eighteen months after starting the work; I think if I had come out straight away it would have been a different story, as described in the original No Outsiders book (Moffat, 2015). Children have moved from being cautious about saying the words 'gay' or 'lesbian' two years ago to using the words in context with confidence.

We are not undermining any faith or belief; we are merely teaching children that living in the UK means we can hold different views and different beliefs and still get along. We link this to British values and celebrate those different beliefs; it's what makes the UK a great place to be!

Chapter Five

REINFORCING THE ETHOS AROUND SCHOOL

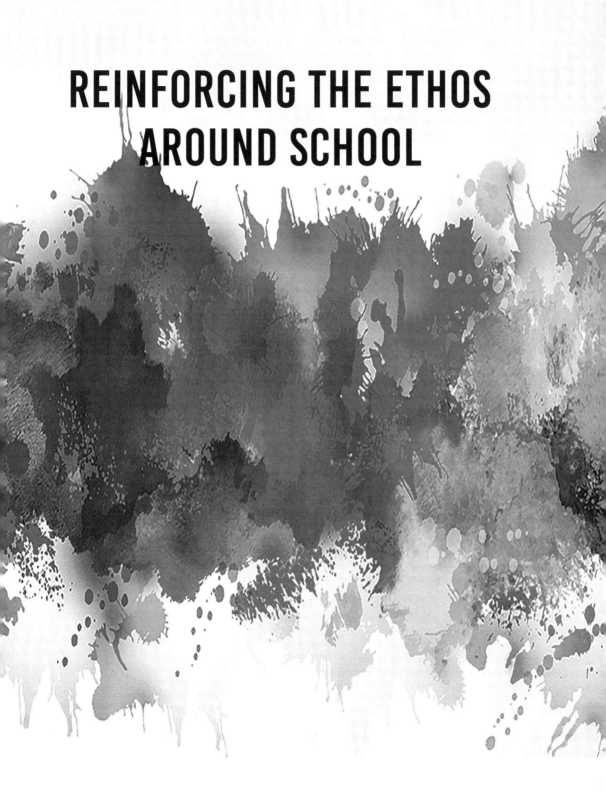

Reinforcing the ethos around school

The lesson plans are only half the job; we need assemblies to reference 'No Outsiders' every week and displays around school. I have included some examples of the school environment here:

Figure 5.1: Parkfield Community School's "This is our school" display

Based on the Michael Rosen book *This Is Our House* (2007), comments from the children written on the display include, "I am British and Pakistani and part of Parkfield Community School. I like being British."

These No Outsiders posters are placed in weather-proof casing and placed at every entrance to the school. Around the poster are quotes from the current Year 6 pupils.

Figure 5.2: Parkfield Community School's "No Outsiders" poster

Sample quote: "Everyone is welcome at Parkfield no matter if they are black, white, a Christian, gay or lesbian."

Situated in the main corridor, this links 'No Outsiders' to anti-bullying and uses the Stonewall 'no bystanders' tag line. Every child in the school has signed the pledge to stand up to bullying and make sure there are no outsiders.

Figure 5.3: Parkfield Community School's "No Outsiders – No bullies" display

Figure 5.4: Parkfield Community School's Year 6 "I can be anything I want to be" display

Inspired by the book *Freedom to Dream* used as a No Outsiders lesson in Year 6, the children have written on the wings of the chair, "It's ok to be . . ." and also on each flower petal what they want to be when they grow up. The heading reads, "My wings will grow in Year 6, I can be anything I want to be."

Figure 5.5: Parkfield Community School's "Exterminate discrimination" display

Combining a Dr Who topic with No Outsiders, a Year 6 class used *My Princess Boy* by Cheryl Kilodavis to write about trans children being welcome in our school.

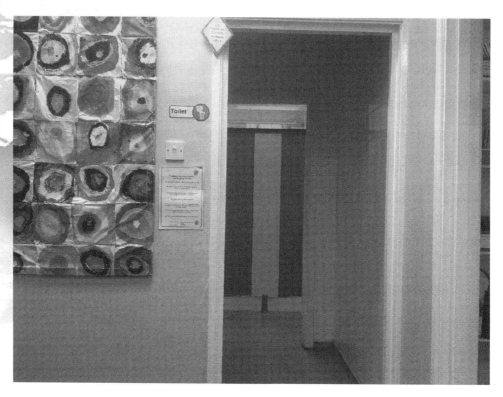

Figure 5.6: Parkfield Community School's gender-neutral toilet

This gender-neutral toilet is situated off the corridor in the centre of the school. No fuss is made about it; it simply provides children with another option. Children can use the boys' toilets or the girls' toilets or this toilet which is for any child. Having a gender-neutral toilet removes the stress for any child questioning their gender identity over which toilet to use. One term after the toilet was introduced, I did a Pupil Voice exercise about school facilities and included a question about which was the preferred toilet that children used. Many said they like this one and when I asked why, expecting answers about it being safe or children feeling secure, all of them said they used it because "it was closest". Children really are unfussed about these things!

Figure 5.7: Parkfield Community School's parent art work

Our coffee morning group of mums have been making No Outsiders sewing cushions. They talk about No Outsiders and link the ethos to their own experiences; they have created a multi-language display where they talk about where they were born and where they live now, celebrating being British.

Chapter Six

THE RESOURCE

The resource

Table 6.1: Book list EYFS–Y6

EYFS workshop	*A Busy Day for Birds* – Lucy Cousins
Year 1 workshop 1	*Under the Same Sky* – Britta Teckentrup
Year 1 workshop 2	*Spacegirl Pukes* – Katy Watson
Year 2 workshop 1	*My Friend Jamal* – Anna Quin
Year 2 workshop 2	*The Bear Who Stared* – Duncan Beedie
Year 3 workshop 1	*Ice in the Jungle* – Ariane Hofman-Maniyar
Year 3 workshop 2	*My Name Is Not Refugee* – Kate Milner
Year 4 workshop 1	*Last Stop on Market Street* – Matt De La Pena
Year 4 workshop 2	*Odd Dog Out* – Rob Biddulph
Year 5 workshop 1	*Welcome* – Barroux
Year 5 workshop 2	*Stella Brings the Family* – Miriam B Schiffer
Year 6 workshop 1	*The Journey* – Francesca Sanna
Year 6 workshop 2	*Du Iz Tak?* – Carson Ellis

Table 6.2: EYFS children and parents session 1

Text: *A Busy Day for Birds* – Lucy Cousins
Aim: To celebrate our differences LI: To celebrate difference
Intro: Put the inside cover of *A Busy Day for Birds* on the board and ask children with their adult to choose one of the birds they see and think of three words to describe it. Ask a child to describe a bird to the group and ask others to point to the bird the child is describing.
Read *A Busy Day for Birds* start to finish without stopping for comments. At the end of the story ask the following questions: • What's this book about? • What are the birds doing? • Are all the birds in the book the same or are they all different? • In what ways are the birds different?
Role play: Explain we are going to be the birds in the book. Encourage the adults to join in with their child. We are all going to be birds for the day! Go through the book again, but this time every time an action is described encourage the children and their adult to join in ('hop hop hop', 'flap your wings', 'stretch up your neck' etc.). The last action is to cuddle with 'Mum' (adult) and then fall asleep. Give the group a clap; say they were brilliant! Just like the birds in the book!
Main activity: Ask each child and adult to draw/paint a bird of their choice; it may be a bird from the story or it may be a completely new bird. Say you want to see if we all draw birds that look the same or if we draw and colour birds that look different. Say you are excited to see what we all come up with.
Plenary: Show the art work and highlight/praise the different colours, shapes and sizes. Say you are really pleased because this shows we all like difference and we don't have to be all the same. Say this art work reminds you of the people in this room – we all have differences too: skin, hair, shapes and sizes. We are just like the birds in this book – all different and having a great day together! Look again at the inside cover of the book and at all the different birds; are any birds left out? We can see they are all different and they are all flying together, living together. Just like us!
Homework: Give children an image of three outlines of different-shaped birds sitting next to each other on a branch. The child and adult should colour in the birds using different colours. Say you want to see the different birds together. The birds like being with other birds who are different.

Table 6.3: Y1 children and parents session 1

Text: *Under the Same Sky* – Britta Teckentrup
Aim: To appreciate and welcome difference
LI: To investigate similarities and differences
Intro: Display two different animals. With their adult partner, children come up with similarities and differences. Feedback to class.
Read *Under the Same Sky* all the way through without stopping or commenting. At the end, put the first question on the board and ask children and adult to discuss. Discuss three questions one at a time and feedback to the class: • What different animals were in the story? • What different places were in the story? • What do the different animals share?
Main activity: Explain we are going to play a game all about similarities and differences. Show the group a large dice with words written on each face; three faces have 'same' written on them and three faces have 'different' written on them. Ask for a child to come to the front and choose another child as a volunteer. The children throw the dice and if it lands on 'different' they identify a difference between them; if the dice lands on 'same' the children identify something about them that is the same. Repeat with different pairs and then ask adults to have a go; will an adult come to the front and choose another to play with? Reinforce there are lots of ways we are different and also lots of ways we are the same; do we get along? Yes! It's ok to be different; you can still be friends!
Art activity: Look again at the final picture in the book where all the animals sit under the same sky together. Each child paints themselves with their adult under the sky and then adds other people or animals. The aim is to create a picture where different people and animals can be seen sharing the same sky together.
Plenary: Why is the last picture in the story like us? It's like us because we are all different and we share the same sky too. We have different skin, different hair and different clothes, we look different and some of our lives are different, but we share the same sky and we get on. Say that's why we say there are no outsiders, because we know people in our school are different but no one is left out.
Homework: Under a No Outsiders moon, children draw four different animals sitting together.

Table 6.4: Y1 children and parents session 2

Text: *Spacegirl Pukes* – Katy Watson (illustrated by Vanda Carter)
Aim: To challenge gender stereotypes LI: To work with different families
Intro: Tell the group that today we are going to talk about space travel and astronauts. Ask each pair to draw an astronaut in their rocket in space. As each pair are drawing, go round and ask children about their astronaut – what is your astronaut's name? Why do they like being an astronaut? Ask everyone to show their pictures. Did anyone draw a female astronaut? Show a picture of a female astronaut.
Read *Spacegirl Pukes* start to finish without stopping for comments. Then encourage discussion between each child and parent in the following questions: • What happens to Spacegirl? • Why do all the other characters get sick too? • Who helps Spacegirl get better? • What do you think she will find on her travels in space?
Role play: Act out the story as a whole group, asking all the children to be spaceboys and spacegirls. Put the adults behind desks and explain they all work in the control tower. Now read through the story again; have each child being sick over their adult at the start and then have the adult care for the child as in the book – hugging and putting to bed. Then – oh no! – all the adults are sick too! Have the adults sitting with their child being ill. Ask for someone to be the cat and be sick in the middle of the room too. Then the child feels better and the adult is the ground crew helping the space girl/boy to put on the space suit . . . oops. The ground controller is sick too! It's time to go – each adult hugs their child goodbye and everyone counts down 10–1 . . . but there's no petrol! Each spacegirl and spaceboy fills their rocket with petrol and we count down again before each child blasts off and we wave goodbye as they fly around the room.
Main activity: What happens next? Children draw their rocket in space or on the moon. Adults help to draw stars and planets. Perhaps there are aliens to meet!
Plenary: Say you really enjoyed our role play because everyone joined in and we had fun together. In the story, who was in Spacegirl's family? (Spacegirl, Mummy Louka, Mummy Neenee). Who is in your family? It's great that today all the different families joined in together in our role play.
Homework: Some people might think all astronauts are boys, but we know boys and girls can go into space. Draw two astronauts on the moon next to their space rocket. Write their names, to show one is a boy and one is a girl.

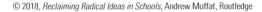

Table 6.5: Y2 children and parents session 1

Text: *My Friend Jamal* – Anna Quin

Aim: To exchange dialogue about difference

LI: To ask questions

Intro: Put the word "Britain" on the board. Ask each child and their adult to talk about who lives in Britain today. Is everyone the same? In what ways are people living in Britain today different from each other?

Read *My Friend Jamal* start to finish without stopping for comments. Now put up the following questions on the board for discussion and then feedback as a group:

- In what ways are Joseph and Jamal similar?

- In what ways are Joseph and Jamal different?

- How are the boys' homes different?

- What did Joseph learn at the party about clothes?

- Why does Joseph ask Jamal's mum lots of questions?

- Is Jamal's mum happy to answer questions? Why?

- What can we learn from Joseph in this story?

Main activity: Our job today is to find out about the different adults in our room. You may know some adults here today or you may not know anyone. Today you are going to find answers to three questions:

- Have you always lived in _____ (insert city)? If not, where else have you lived?

- What languages can you speak?

- What was your first pet?

- What is your favourite food?

Put coloured tokens or cubes into a hat and ask each pair to randomly pick one. Then each pair finds another pair with the same colour cube and talk to each other. Express you want the child to lead the questions to each adult, but adults can join in once the question has been asked. You are welcome to ask more questions if you wish. You might also want to start by introducing yourself and asking your adult's name. Swap groups around so that people get to talk to different people.

Plenary: Get the group back together and ask if anyone found out anything new today about anyone. Did anyone find they had things in common with anyone? In the story Jamal gets to learn lots about his friend's family; how does he find out? Why do you think it's good to ask questions and find out new things? Some people are frightened of new things, different things or change. What advice would you give if someone was frightened of difference? (talk/exchange dialogue)

Homework: Your task is to find an adult in school this week and ask them our four questions. You can't choose someone in our own class. Find out something new about someone.

Table 6.6: Y2–1 worksheet

I talked to _____
• Have you always lived here? If not, where else have you lived?
• What languages can you speak?
• What was your first pet?
• What is your favourite food?

Table 6.7: Y2 children and parents session 2

Text: *The Bear Who Stared* – Duncan Beedie
Aim: To make conversation with a stranger
LI: To say "Hello"
Intro: Put the front cover of the book up on the board and ask the group to talk in their pairs about what the bear is staring at and why he might be staring. Come up with two different scenarios for why the bear is staring. Ask for a few pairs to feedback their ideas. Did anyone have the same ideas?
Read *The Bear Who Stared* start to finish without stopping for comments. Now ask the group again why the bear was staring (he was shy). Put up the following questions for discussion and then feedback: • How did the other animals feel when Bear stared at them? • What explanation did Bear give for why he stares? • What advice did Frog give? • What changes for Bear when he takes the advice?
Main activity: Explain we are going to play 'Musical smiles'. It's like musical statues but instead of standing still when the music stops, in this game when the music stops everyone gives the person next to them the widest smile they can and says, "Hello!" What do adults often do when they meet someone? They shake hands; if adults wish they can shake hands too. In this game no one is out for smiling last; and if you happen to stop near two people you can say hello twice or even three times. Let's make sure in our game that no one is left out! What else could you say after, "Hello!"? How about, "My name is _____." Play music and encourage the group to move around the room, stopping and greeting each time the music stops. Give adults a target – by the end of the game the winner is the person who has greeted the most people.
Plenary: How did you feel the first time the music stopped? Did saying hello get easier the more you did it? What was the atmosphere in the room like at the end of the game? How is everyone feeling now? Have we made a happy space? If we see someone who looks different sometimes we stare at them. What can we learn from this book? How can we make our community a place where everyone feels welcome?
Homework: See worksheet. Explain tomorrow you want the adult and child to think about all the people they say hello to that day. Who can name the most people? Make it a competition. On the sheet there is a box for the adult and a box for the child to draw and label their people.

Table 6.8: Y2–2 worksheet

Today I said "Hello" to . . .
_____
Today I said "Hello" to . . .
_____

Table 6.9: Y3 children and parents session 1

Text: *Ice in the Jungle* – Ariane Hofman-Maniyar
Aim/LI: To adapt to change
Intro: Put the words "Ice in the jungle" on the board without showing the image on the front cover of the book: what does the title make you think of? In what parts of the world do we find ice? Why don't we usually find ice in jungles? Ask children with their adult to think of three words to describe the climate in a jungle and the climate in the North/South Pole. How would an animal travelling from one climate to the other feel?
Read *Ice in the Jungle* all the way through without stopping or commenting. At the end ask the group, what different feelings does Ice experience in the book? Put the following questions on the board and encourage children and adults to discuss each one before a feedback and discussion as a whole group. • Why does everyone stare at Ice when she first goes to school? • Ice can't understand when everyone asks her questions; what else could they do? • How does Ice try to make new friends? What are the animals doing? • Why do the animals have a North Pole party? • What do you think is the effect of the party on Ice? • What do you think is the effect of the party on the animals? (They get to learn about a different place.) • Is the class better for having Ice in it? Why?
Main activity: If someone new joined our school from a different place with a different language, how would we make them feel welcome? We are not told in the story where the character Ice comes from. For the purpose of the role play say Ice comes from Svalbard, situated mid-way between mainland Norway and the North Pole and home to approximately 3,000 polar bears. The official language of Svalbard is Norwegian. Ask if anyone in the room speaks Norwegian and if so, they can help with the activity. Explain we are going to hold a celebration to welcome our new classmate from Svalbard. Look at the example given in the book; how could the sign be improved for Ice? (It is in English; it could be written in a language Ice understands.)

Table 6.9 (continued)

Split the group into groups of 6–8 and give each group a different task:

1. Make a large flag of Svalbard (Norwegian flag).

2. Make a large sign in Norwegian saying, "Welcome to our school" (Velkommen til skolen vår). Another sign could read, "Everyone welcome here" (alle velkommen her).

3. Paint landscape pictures of Svalbard (find images on the internet).

4. Paint examples of other marine life found in Svalbard: whales, dolphins, seals, walruses.

5. Polar bears eat mainly seals. We don't have a supply of seals to offer to Ice, so paint examples of dishes she may like to try here.

Plenary: Why did Ice and her mum move from home? What reasons do people have for moving to a different country? Is moving always a choice? When may moving not be a choice? How would you feel if you had to move to a different country, learn a new language and adapt? Has anyone here had that experience? Encourage sharing of experiences; did anyone do something that made life easier?

Homework: Today we painted a Norwegian flag. What does a UK flag look like? Why do countries have their own flags? At what sort of celebrations do we see people waving flags? What other flags do you know? Draw the UK flag and two others for your homework.

Table 6.10: Y3–1 worksheet

Name of country
Draw the flag

Name of country
Draw the flag

Name of country
Draw the flag

Table 6.11: Y3 children and parents session 2

Text: *My Name Is Not Refugee* – Kate Milner
Aim: To consider attitudes towards refugees
LI: To consider why names are important
Intro: Put the word "Refugee" on the board. What does the word make you think of? What is a refugee? What does a refugee need?
Read *My Name Is Not Refugee*. There are questions on each page; ask for volunteers to answer each question as you read through the book. At the end ask the group, what different feelings does the child in the book experience? Put the following questions on the board and encourage children and adults to discuss each one before a feedback and discussion as a whole group. • What new experiences does the child in the story have? • Which experiences would you find difficult? • How do you think Mum feels when she can't understand words or when she has to sleep in strange places? • What makes the child happy at the end? • How do you think the child feels when called a refugee?
Main activity: Why does Mum say, "You'll be called Refugee, but Refugee is not your name"? Why are names important? Ask every child and adult in the room to write their name on a piece of card and place it in a bowl in the middle of the room. Now explain we all have names and all our names are in the bowl. Names are very important because they give us our identity and make us different. Explain we are going to perform a naming ceremony. Show the group a 'naming hat'. We take turns to wear the naming hat and approach the bowl, take a card and read the name aloud. We identify the person the name belongs to and we approach them, bow and say, "Welcome _____ you belong here!" The hat then goes to the person who has been named, who approaches the bowl and takes a different name. Continue till everyone is named.
Art activity: Each child and adult creates a name painting using their name. Make the names bright and colourful and individual.

Table 6.11 (continued)

Plenary: Recap, why are names important? In the story, why does Mum want her child to remember their name? In our role play, why was it important to say "You belong here" to everyone using their names? What do we say in our school about where people belong?

Look at the page at the end of the book where the strange words start to make sense; why are they starting to make sense? What has the child's school done to make sure the child feels they belong? If a new child came to our school who used a different language or looked different, what would we do?

Homework: If a new child comes to our school with a different language, we need to have things in place to help them to learn English. Divide a sheet of A4 into six and in each box draw and label one object you think might help the child to learn English. If your new friend doesn't know the word for toilet, they could point to a picture of a toilet and you could teach them the word. Draw a toilet and label it for them. What other objects/words might be useful?

Table 6.12: Y4 children and parents session 1

Text: *Last Stop on Market Street* – Matt De La Pena
Aim: To recognise and celebrate diversity LI: To investigate diversity in my class
Intro: Write "diversity" on the board and ask children and their adult to discuss and come up with a definition for the word. Are we diverse in this room? Can you tell a group is diverse by just looking at them? Why not?
Read *Last Stop on Market Street* all the way through without stopping or commenting. When finished, put the following questions on the board and ask each child with their adult to discuss before feedback: • What does CJ learn on his journey? • Why do you think Nana takes CJ to the soup kitchen every week? • Could this story setting work in our city? What is the same, what is different? • Why is this book about diversity? • How many different people can you remember from the story?
Main activity: In the story, CJ and Nana travel on a bus and meet lots of different people. Look at the page where Nana and CJ get on the bus; what does Nana do when she gets on the bus? (She says "good afternoon" and smiles at people.) Why does she do that? What similarities do people have on the bus? What differences are there? Explain we are going to role play the bus. How can we make this room look more like a bus? Work as a team to create a bus using chairs. Now ask who was on the bus? Many different people got on the bus in the story; can we find ways we are different to act out the story? Give out sticky labels and ask each child and adult to think of a way they are different from others in the room; think of ethnicities, cultures, family, ages, abilities, genders, experiences, hobbies, talents etc. Can we think of differences for everyone here? Ask for someone to be the driver who sits at the front, now ask everyone to wear their labels with pride and one by one get on the bus. When they get on the bus, people must do as Nana did, saying hello to everyone as they find their seat. When everyone is on the bus, explain you are the ticket inspector. The label is the ticket; walk down the bus collecting labels and commenting on each, saying, "Welcome!" When all labels have been collected, announce, "Last stop on Market Street" and help everyone off the bus.
Art activity: Adult and child together make a flower to use in our homework. Encourage 3D flowers.

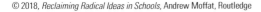

Table 6.12 (continued)

Plenary: Hold up the labels you collected on the role play up and ask the group, "Do we need these labels?" What shall we do with them? We could put them up in our classroom to show we are proud of our differences, or we could throw them away because we don't need them; we all know who we are and everyone is accepted. What do people want to do? Have a group discussion and a vote.
Homework: In the story, CJ and Nana go to a soup kitchen to help others in their community. The homework is to perform a random act of kindness for someone on your street. Use the flowers and explain the homework is to visit someone on their street after school, give them the flower and say, "I hope you have a nice day."

Table 6.13: Y4 children and parents session 2

Text: *Odd Dog Out* – Rob Biddulph
Aim: To encourage individuality LI: To be unafraid of difference
Intro: Put up an image of the city centre where the school is. The image needs to show people. Ask the group to look at the image and note down with their partner all the differences they see in the people. Is everyone the same or is everyone different? How are people different?
Read *Odd Dog Out* all the way through without stopping or commenting. At the end, ask the group to discuss and feedback the following questions: • Why does dog leave her town? • How does she feel when she sees a hundred others just like her? • Why does dog feel sorry at first for the dog who stands out? • Dog uses the word 'outsider'; what is an outsider? • What does dog learn in this story? • What do the dogs back home say when dog returns? What have they started to do? Why?
Main activity: Sometimes people are scared of standing out and being treated like an outsider. At our school we say there are no outsiders; everyone is welcome and it's ok to be different. Show the group a range of hats and assorted decorations. Explain you want dog to realise she could come to our school and we would accept her difference. We are all going to make a unique hat to celebrate difference in our school. Encourage everyone to make their own hat with colours and decorations. At the end of the session take a group photo (and tweet it – no outsiders at our school: we love being different!).
Plenary: Recap and discuss what the story is about; does it have a message? What is the message? In the story the second dog says, "stand tall, be proud" – is this the message? Look again at the last page; what does "blaze a trail. Be who you are" mean? How is this book a No Outsiders story?
Homework: Give the group worksheet Y4–2. Around the words "Blaze a trail. Be who you are", children and their adult should draw outlines of themselves and label ways they are different and proud; encourage children and adults to label likes, hobbies, achievements, faith, culture etc.

Table 6.14: Y4–1 worksheet

Blaze a trail.

Be who you are.

Table 6.15: Y5 children and parents session 1

Text: *Welcome* – Barroux
LI: To investigate responses to refugees
Intro: What is a refugee? Put the word on the board and ask each child and their adult to come up with a definition. Feedback and come up with an agreed definition as a group.
Read *Welcome* start to finish, then ask children to write down the responses given to the polar bears each time they ask to live on an island. What did the other animals say? Write the animal responses on the board for use in the role play. • Why were the polar bears asking for a place to live? • Did the polar bears want to leave their home? • What happened to the ice? (It became unsafe and they had to leave.) • How do you think the polar bears felt as they left?
Main activity: Look at the responses given by the animals when the polar bears ask to land on each island. Use worksheet Y5–1 to respond to each line. If you were there, what could you say to the animals? Would you agree or would you try and change their minds? Children and adults discuss and fill in the boxes together.
Art activity: Child and adult paint together an island with different animals living together. There needs to be a sign saying "Welcome" somewhere on the island.
Plenary: Consider what it would be like to live on each of the three islands in the story. One island has just cows living on it, one has just a panda on it and one has just giraffes on it. The last island has polar bears and monkeys living on it, and they say people are 'welcome'. Which island do you think would be the best place to live? Why? Think about the UK today; are we all the same or are we all different? If we were all the same and we all came from the same place, what would our life be like? Who likes pizza? Where was pizza invented? Where was the first play station invented? (Japan) Football is believed to have originated in Egypt. What benefits are there from a diverse world where people can meet new people?
Homework: Research with your adult to find where things on worksheet Y5–2 originated.

Table 6.16: Y5–1 worksheet

Write responses to each of the animal comments. You can agree or disagree with the animals.

The polar bears ask, "Please can we live here?"
The cows reply, "You are too tall, you are too furry."
You say:
The panda replies, "Hmmm, you are too many."
You say:
The giraffes reply, "Did you hear something?"
"That's too much bother."
You say:
Your message to the polar bears:

Table 6.17: Y5–2 worksheet

What are the benefits of meeting and working with different people?
Where did the following originate?
Where was Chicken Tikka Masala invented?
Who invented the iPad and where did they live?
When/where was ice cream first eaten?
Who invented crisps (potato chips)?
Who built the first car in 1769?
Where was chocolate first used?
What did Baron Karl von Drais design in 1818 and where did he live?

Table 6.18: answer sheet Y5–3

What are the benefits of meeting and working with different people?
Where did the following originate?
Answer sheet
Where was Chicken Tikka Masala invented?
Thought to have originated in an Indian restaurant in Glasgow or from the British Bangladeshi community living in the UK.
Where was the iPad invented?
San Francisco, USA
When/where was ice cream first eaten?
Ancient Greeks ate snow mixed with honey in 5 BC.
Who invented crisps (potato chips)?
George Crum invented the potato chip. He was Native American/African American and lived in New York.
Who built the first car in 1769?
Nicholas Joseph Cugnot built the first car in Paris.
Where was chocolate first used?
Mexico
What did Baron Karl von Drais design in 1818 and where was he from?
German inventor of the bicycle.

Table 6.19: Y5 children and parents session 2

Text: *Stella Brings the Family* – Miriam B Schiffer
Aim: To ensure all families feel welcome in schools
LI: To make our school inclusive
Intro: Put the word "inclusion" on the board without showing the image on the front cover of the book. Ask children and their adult to come up with a definition for the word. Share some definitions, write down ideas; identify one definition as a group.
Read *Stella Brings the Family* all the way through without stopping or commenting. At the end ask the group, why is this book about no outsiders? Put the following questions on the board for children to discuss with their adult and then feedback to the group. • Why does Stella feel like an outsider? • Why does Stella invite so many people to Mother's day? • Why doesn't Stella's teacher say no? • What do you think the school needs to do in the future to make sure everyone feels welcome?
Main activity: Look at the last page where a girl with two mums thinks about a Father's day party. How is she feeling? What needs to happen at that school to make sure no one feels like an outsider? Ask each child and adult to make a new invite for the Mothers' day party. But this time make it inclusive. Check everyone knows what inclusive means; the aim is to create an invitation where no one feels like an outsider. Or ask everyone to paint a "real families" poster, using their family as a model and labelling the people. Reinforce the fact that everyone has different families and everyone is welcome.
Plenary: When we invited everyone today, did we say the session was just for mums? Why did we say "parents/carers"? Look at the story about the single mum living in America who dressed up as dad to support her son at "Donuts with Dad day" (Amy Packham, *Huffington Post*, 17/02/17). Why did she do that? How can schools make sure everyone feels welcome and there are no outsiders? Is our school inclusive? What is the law in the UK about discrimination? (The Equality Act 2010) What groups are included in the Equality Act? (See preface at start of this book.) Where does Stella's family fit into the Equality Act 2010?
Homework: Some people don't know about No Outsiders so we need to tell them. We need everyone to know about equality and diversity so that stories like this one don't happen in the future. How many people can you speak to about No Outsiders and the Equality Act tonight? Ask everyone you speak to for a signature; who can speak to the most people?

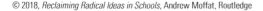

Table 6.20: Y5–4 worksheet

Spread the No Outsiders message	
I told _____ people about the Equality Act and No Outsiders	
Person	**Signature**

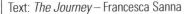

Table 6.21: Y6 children and parents session 1

Text: *The Journey* – Francesca Sanna
Aim/LI: To consider the experiences of migrants and refugees
Intro: Put the book cover on the board and ask each child and adult to study the image. What do they see? What is it about? What's happening? What are the emotions evoked from the image?
Read *The Journey* start to finish without commenting or stopping. At the end of the story, ask children and their adults to talk about the story and its illustrations. Put the following points on the board to discuss. Feedback for a whole-group discussion. • Who is telling the story? We are never told their name; why do you think this is? • Why does the narrator leave home? • Explain this line: "The further we go . . . the more we leave behind." • Why do the children think Mother is never scared? Is Mother scared? • Why does the family keep travelling and crossing borders? • What do you think about the ending?
Main activity: Look at the picture accompanying the words "Since that day everything has become darker and my mother has become more and more worried." What do you see in the picture? Does the family feel safe staying where they are? Why does Mother say leaving will be a "great adventure"? Think about the group of people in this classroom now; who feels safe? What makes you feel safe right now? Ask children and their adult to think about what things make them feel safe now. On slips of paper ask each pair to write what makes them feel safe. Show a large bowl; explain this is our 'safety bowl'. Ask for a child to read out their words and place the paper in the bowl, before taking it to another child who reads their words and places them in the bowl. Continue until everyone's words are in the bowl. It's ok if some of the words people read out are repeated. You want everyone to have thought about what makes them feel safe today. When the bowl is full, thank everyone and say you will keep it in the classroom to remind us all how safe we are, because not everyone in the world today feels the same way.
Plenary: Some people say migrants and refugees are not welcome and should 'go back' or go somewhere else. Some people say that if you are different or have different skin colour or language or culture that you don't belong. What do we say in our school? We say there are no outsiders; why do we say that? We don't know where the family in the story ends up; if the children came to our school tomorrow how does 'No Outsiders' help? What does the Equality Act say about people who are different? What does the UN Convention on the rights of a child say about refugee children? (See Article 22.)
Homework: Research the UN Convention on the rights of a child; what is it, when was it created, who is it for? Write an explanation illustrating ways the declaration helps to make people safe.

Table 6.22: Y6 children and parents session 2

Text: *Du Iz Tak?* – Carson Ellis
Aim/LI: To explore and embrace different languages
Intro: How many languages do we have in this room? Does anyone speak languages other than English? Do a count and if people do speak other languages, ask them to say a sentence. Express your admiration that a person in our school has two languages!
Note: practice reading this book aloud before the session Read *Du Iz Tak?* start to finish and then ask the group what they thought happened in the story. Children and adult should discuss and come up with a brief synopsis and then feedback. Does anyone recognise the language used in the story? Say you will tell people what the language is at the end of the session. In child/adult pairs, discuss and then feedback. • How did it feel to hear a story in a new language? • Did you understand what was happening? • Did the language get easier to understand the more you read/heard? • Were you able to translate any of the words?
Main activity: Explain the language in the story is made up. The aim is to explore how we can work together when language is a barrier. Can we work together if we speak different languages? Put people into groups of four (or two family groups) and give them a task to create a completely new language for counting to ten. Emphasise using recognised language is not allowed. Can anyone do sums in their new language? How do you say "add" or "take away" and "equals"? Groups may use props to help count. Ask each group to then teach another group to count to ten in their new language.
Plenary: It's good to hear a different language and words that we don't understand. But even though we couldn't understand the characters in the story, did we know what was going on? How? Do we always need common language to communicate? How else can we communicate with someone if we don't have a common language? Tell the story of the girl in California who used Google Translate to speak to a new classmate at lunch (Taylor Pittman, *Huffington Post*, 03/11/16). What do you think was the impact on the new classmate?
Homework: Google Translate a message about No Outsiders into a language of your choice. Have a go reading it out. How many different languages can you translate your No Outsiders message into?

Table 6.23: Y6–1 worksheet

My No Outsiders message in *English*

My No Outsiders message in _____

My No Outsiders message in _____

Appendix

Whole school questionnaires to measure impact

Well-being in school KS1   Date: _____   Class: _____

	Agree	Don't know	Disagree
I feel safe in school.			
I feel happy in school.			
When I arrive at school in the morning, someone will smile at me.			
I know all the people in my class.			
I have friends in my school.			
I enjoy play times and lunch times.			
I know who to talk to if I am worried.			
I know what bullying is and what to do if I see it.			
Adults will listen to me and do something if I tell them about bullying in school.			
Children with a disability are treated equally and fairly in our school.			
I like being in a school where people are different.			
I can get along with people who have a different faith to me.			
I like finding out about other religions.			
I like visiting and exploring different religious buildings.			
I know that some families are different.			
I know what the Equality Act is.			
I know what No Outsiders means.			

Well-being in school KS2   Date: _____   Class: _____

	Agree	Don't know	Disagree
I feel safe in school.			
I feel happy in school.			
When I arrive at school in the morning, someone will smile at me.			
I know all the people in my class.			
I have friends in school.			
I enjoy play times and lunch times.			
I know who to talk to if I am worried.			
I know what bullying is and what to do if I see it.			
Adults will listen to me and do something if I tell them about bullying in school.			
Children with a disability are treated equally and fairly in our school.			
I know what racism is and what to do if I see it.			
I like being in a school where people are different.			
I can get along with people who have a different faith to me.			
I like finding out about other faiths.			
I like visiting and exploring different religious buildings.			
I know that some families are different.			
I know that some people are gay or lesbian in the city where I live.			
I know what the Equality Act is.			
I know what No Outsiders means.			

References

Busby, E. (2017) "Revealed: The spike in hate that followed Brexit and Trump"; *TES*, 05/05/17.

Cox, B. (2017) "We can fight the extremism that killed my wife Jo Cox: Here's how that starts"; *The Guardian*, 24/04/17.

Government Equalities Office (2013) "Equality Act 2010: Guidance", Gov.uk, 27 February, online, www.gov.uk/equality-act-2010-guidanceauthor (accessed July 2017).

Gov.uk (2016) "Ofsted inspection framework", www.gov.uk/handbook-from-september-2015

Heap, S.; Sharratt, N. (2004) *Red rockets and rainbow jelly*; Puffin.

Homeoffice.gov.uk (2011) Public sector: Quick start guide to the Equality Duty https://www.gov.uk/government/publications/public-sector-quick-start-guide-to-the-public-sector-equality-duty (accessed September 2017)

HM Gov (2015) "The Prevent Duty: Departmental advice for schools and childcare providers", www.gov.uk

HM Gov (2016) "Ofsted report Parkfield Community School", 10 May 2016, https://reports.ofsted.gov.uk

Lightfoot, L. (2016) "We respect Islam and gay people: The gay teacher transforming a Muslim school"; *The Guardian*, 15/02/16.

Moffat, A. (2015) *No Outsiders in our school: Teaching the Equality Act in primary schools*; Routledge.

Moffat, A. (2016) "My pupils are young UK Muslims – and they're scared about Trump"; *The Guardian*, 14/11/16.

Pittman, T. (2017) "High school students start club to make sure no one sits alone at lunch"; *Huffington Post*, 13/03/17.

Riley-Smith, B. (2016) "EU referendum: George Osbourne compares Ukip 'Breaking Point' migration poster to Nazi propaganda"; *New Statesman*, 16/06/16.

Rosen, M. (2007) *This is our house*; Walker Books.

Sherwood, H., and Pidd, H. (2017) "Muslims at mosques linked to Khalid Masood fear anti-Islam backlash"; *The Guardian*, 24/03/17.

Slater, C. (2017) "Thousands pack Albert Square to remember Manchester terror attack victims"; *Manchester Evening News*, 23/05/17.

Walker, T. (2016) "Donald Trump wins: Here's what you just voted for, America"; *The Independent*, 09/11/16.

Also by Andrew Moffat, *No Outsiders in Our School* (9781909301726)

This resource provides much needed support for every primary school in the delivery of the objectives outlined in the Equality Act 2010; and in the provision of personal, social, health and economic education (PSHE) for every child.

It provides teachers with a curriculum that promotes equality for all sections of the community so that children leave primary school happy and excited about living in a community full of difference and diversity, whether that difference is through ethnicity, gender, ability, sexual orientation, gender identity, age or religion.

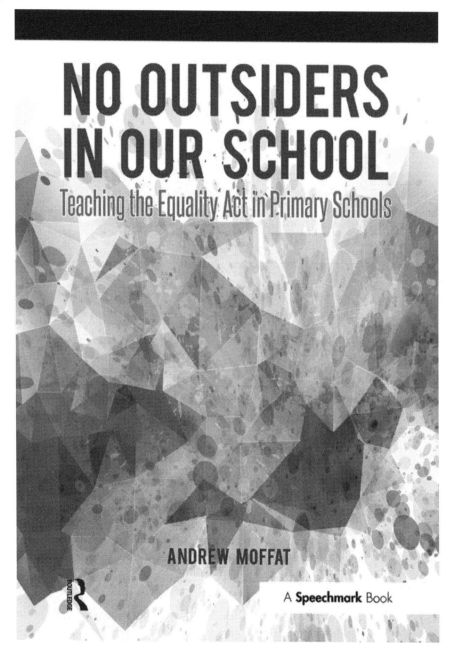

Printed in Great Britain
by Amazon

58773480R00045